HOW TO USE IT?

1. Cut out the page with the chosen stencil, then cut out the stencil leaving around a 1/2" border around the pattern.

2. Tape the stencil to your pumpkin.

3. Using a push pin or needle, poke small holes along the edges of the stencil. Make sure the wholes are closely spaced.

4. Remove the stencil and carve the pumpkin along the dotted lines.

5. If you want to adjust the size of the stencil to your pumpkin, use your copier!

The black area of the stencil is what will be carved out

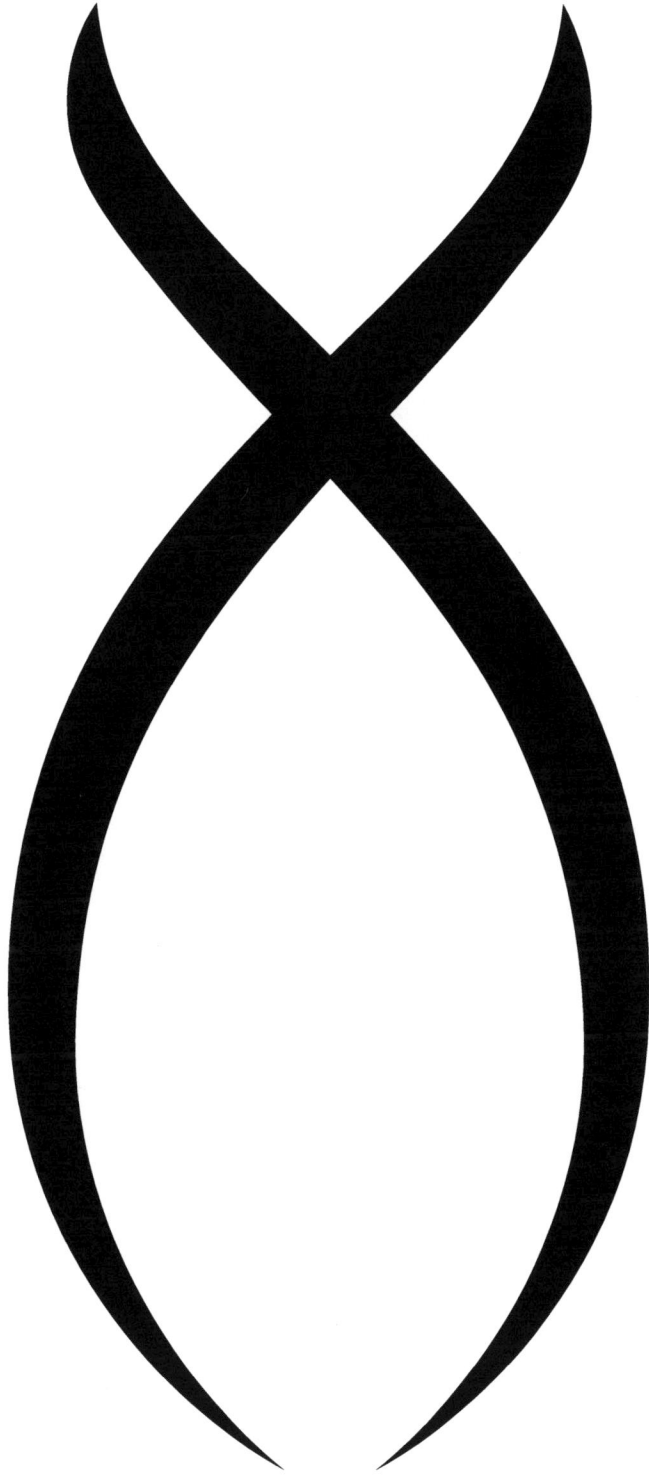

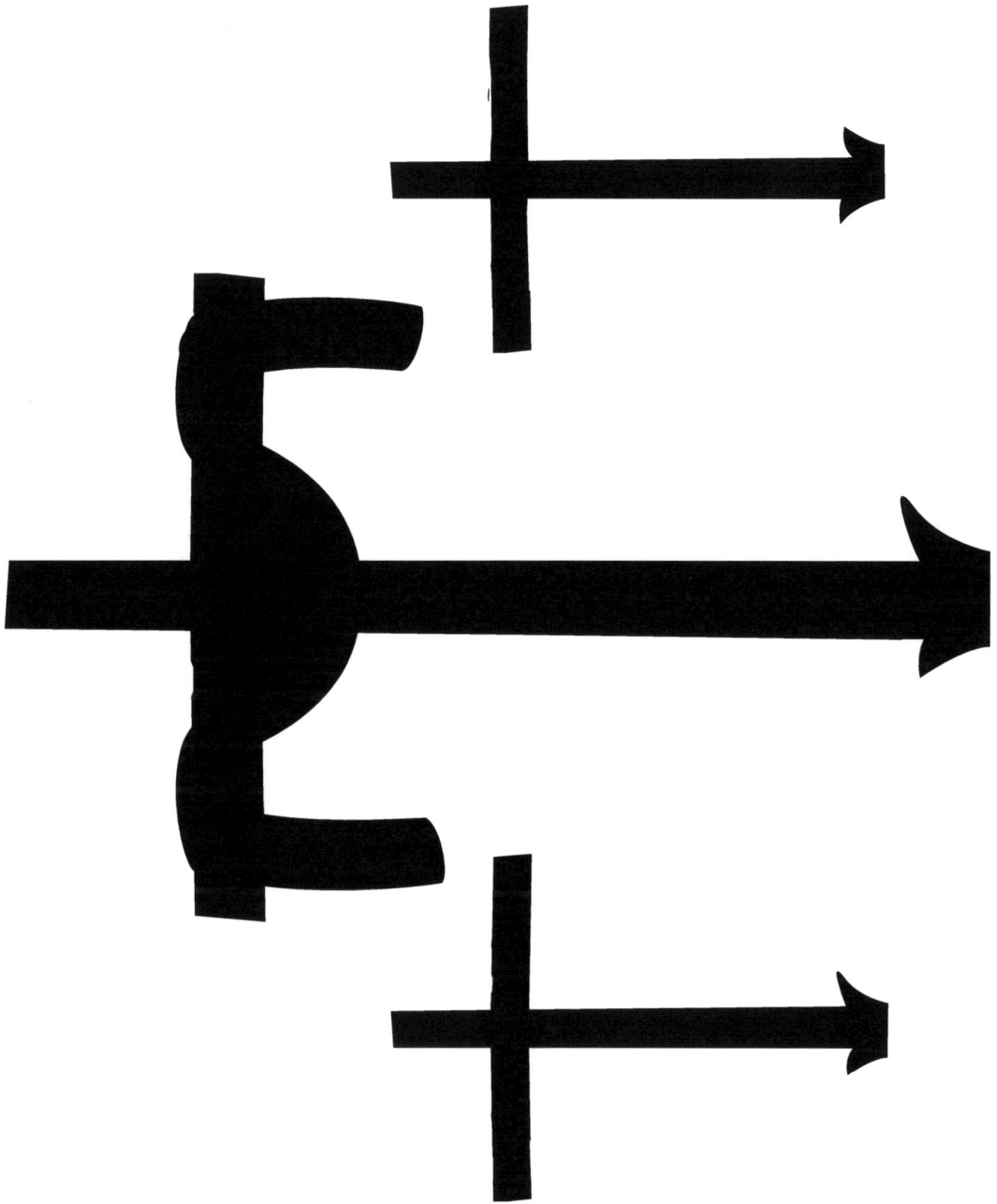

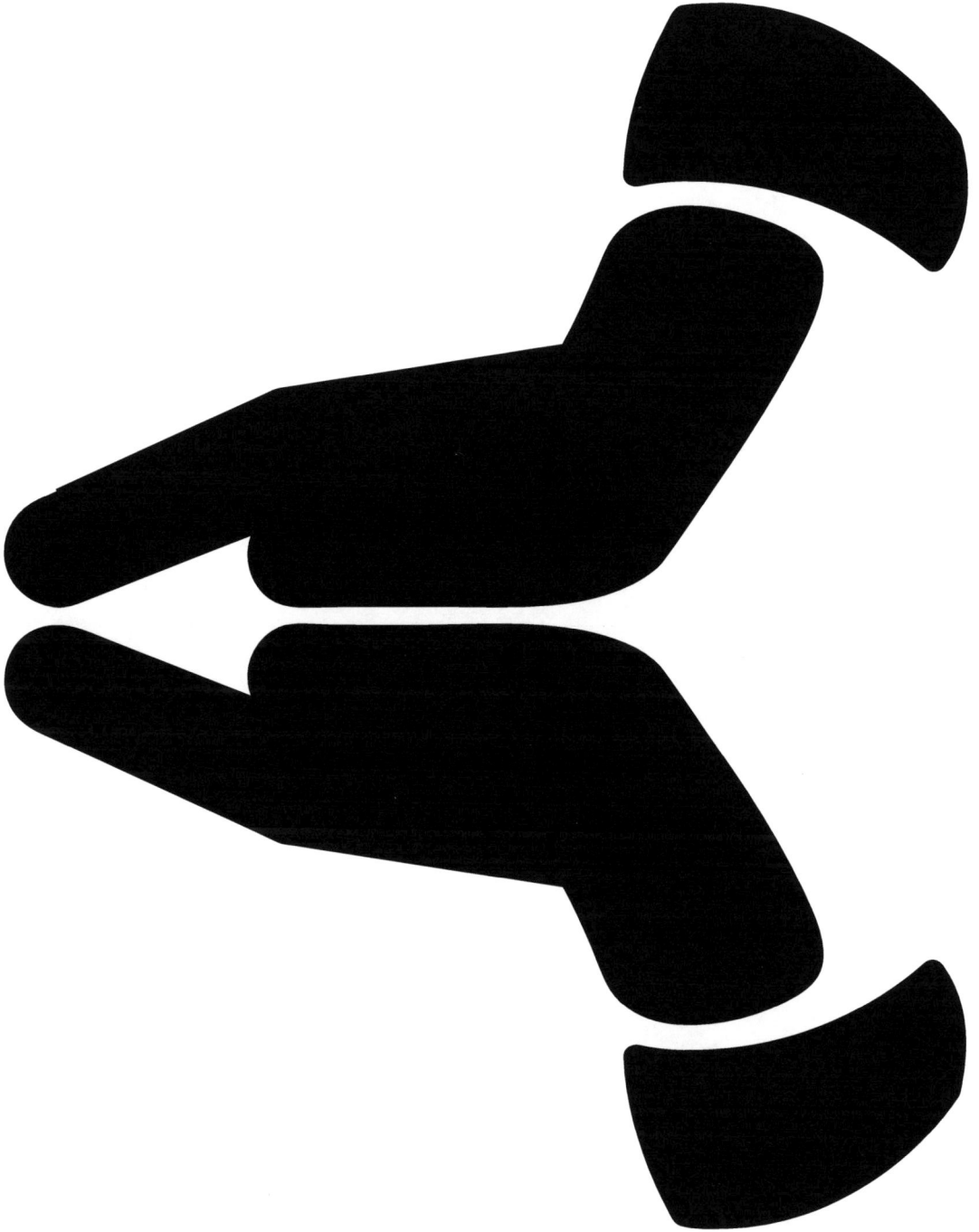

Made in the USA
Las Vegas, NV
29 October 2023